What's it like to be a...

DAIRY FARMER

Written by Susan Cornell Poskanzer
Illustrated by George Ulrich

Troll Associates

Special Consultant: Kris Miller, *Agriculture Instructor, and Future Farmers of America Advisor.*

Library of Congress Cataloging-in-Publication Data

Poskanzer, Susan Cornell.
   Dairy farmer / by Susan Cornell Poskanzer; illustrated by
George Ulrich.
      p.   cm.—(What's it like to be a...)
   Summary: Follows a family of dairy farmers throughout their day as
they tend the cows, operate milking machines, and deliver the milk
to a refrigerated truck which takes it to a dairy plant to be
pasteurized.
   ISBN 0-8167-1426-6 (lib. bdg.)   ISBN 0-8167-1427-4 (pbk.)
   1. Dairy farming—Juvenile literature. 2. Dairy farmers—Juvenile
literature. [1. Dairying. 2. Farmers. 3. Farm life.
4. Occupations.] I. Ulrich, George, ill. II. Title. III. Series.
SF239.5.P67 1989
637'.1—dc19   88-10040

What's it like to be a...
DAIRY FARMER

It is dark and quiet inside the great red barn.
Some cows chew bits of feed. Cleo the cat chases
a mouse out of the barn.

Holstein Cow

The barn door opens. Jason and Eve, the dairy farmers of Sunrise Farm, look proudly at their forty cows.

"Good morning, Belle," says Eve. She pats a big black and white Holstein cow.

"*Moo*," moans Belle.

Eve and Jason lead six cows at a time to the holding area. Here they wash the cows for milking.

When the cows are clean, Eve leads them to a special room called the milking parlor.

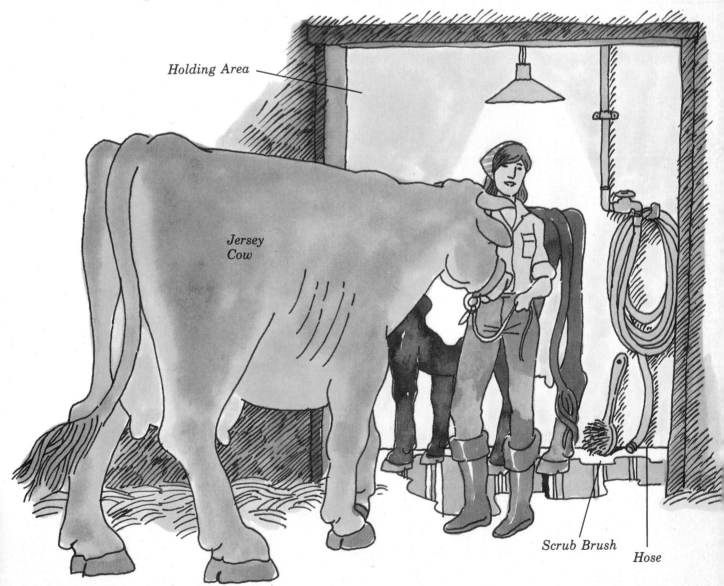

Holding Area

Jersey Cow

Scrub Brush

Hose

In the sparkling clean room, the farmer takes out milking machines.
"Steady, Elizabeth," she tells the cow.

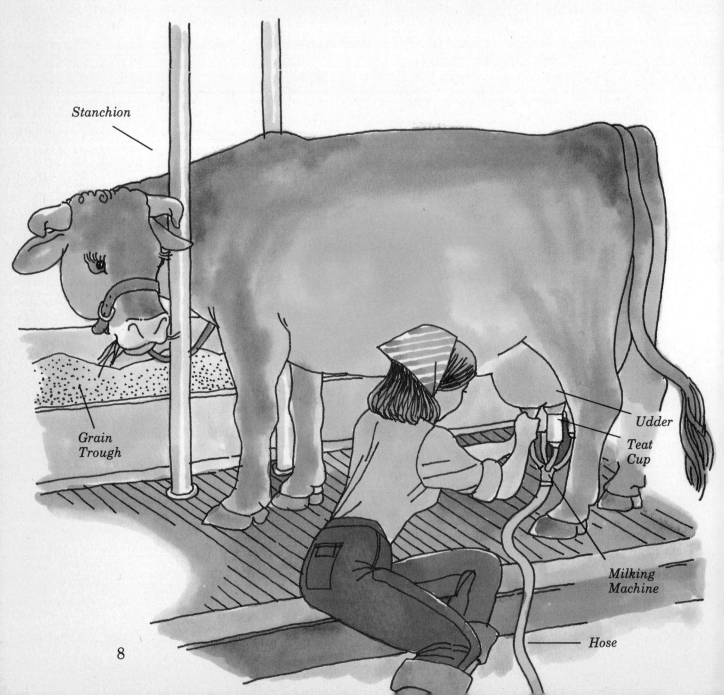

Stanchion

Grain
Trough

Udder

Teat
Cup

Milking
Machine

Hose

Eve attaches the machines and begins milking. After six minutes, Elizabeth has given all her milk. Eve weighs the milk. She notes the amount in a special diary the farmers write in each day. Last year, Elizabeth gave fifteen thousand pounds of milk.

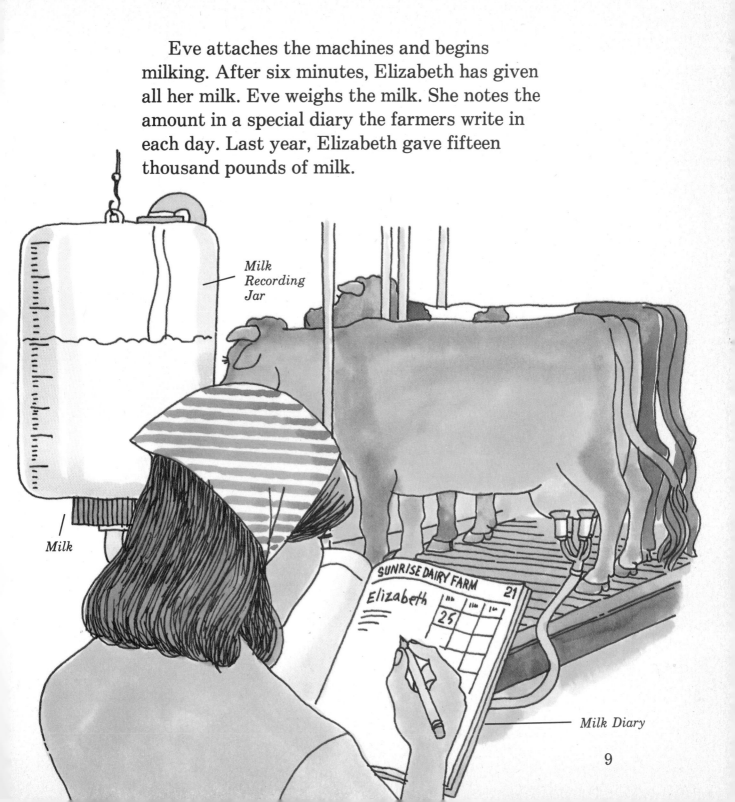

Milk
Recording
Jar

Milk

Milk Diary

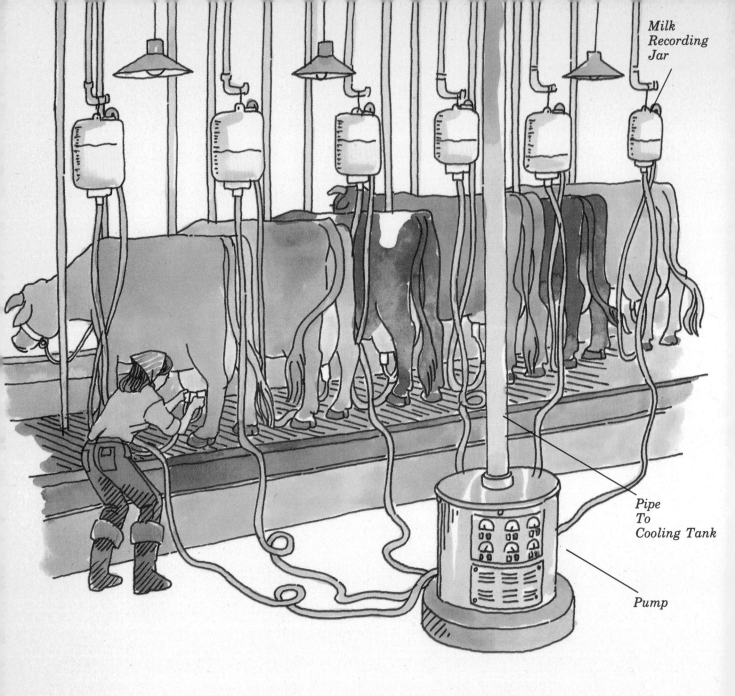

Milk Recording Jar

Pipe To Cooling Tank

Pump

Now it is Henrietta's turn. She is one of the oldest cows. Eve moves quickly from cow to cow, finishing the milking by hand.

The sun rises. The July morning warms up. When the other cows are washed, Jason comes to help with the milking. By seven-thirty, all the cows have been milked.

Pipe To Tank

Stanchion

Recording Jar

Hose

Pump

Eve watches the milk travel from the cows through glass pipes to the milk tank. The milk never touches air. It stays clean and fresh. The milk cools in the tank.

12

Jason and Eve clean the milking equipment and feed the cows.

"I hope Kira is awake," says Eve. "I'm hungry."

Kira is Eve and Jason's daughter. In the farmhouse, she is busily making breakfast.

Hose

Mop

Pail

Jason checks Belle's stanchion, the metal piece that holds her in place in her stall.

"I sure could use some pancakes," he says with a smile.

15

"Me, too," answers Eve.

Inside, Kira flips the last pancake. She sees her parents walk up to the house. Near the barn, she sees her own heifer, Polly. She can't wait to visit the baby cow.

"Good morning, Kira," says Eve. She and Jason smell the warm pancakes and smile at Kira.

"Hi, Mom and Dad," says Kira. "You're just in time!"

"After breakfast, I'm going to town to buy cow feed," says Jason.

The cows eat greens, hay, and corn that grow at Sunrise Farm. They also eat vitamin feed that helps them make more milk.

"Fine," says Eve. "I'll cut hay in the south meadow."

"I'll visit Polly," reports Kira.

"You're doing fine work with her," says Jason. "She's really growing."

"Hi, anybody home?" asks Ken, as he opens the screen door. Ken drives the big truck that brings milk from the farm to the dairy plant.

"How is everything at Sunrise Farm?" says Ken.

Filling Hose

Refrigerated
Tank Truck

Cooling Tank

"Milking went fine this morning," says Eve.
"It's all ready for you."

They go to the milk tank. Milk is pumped into
Ken's shiny refrigerator truck. Jason marks the
amount in the diary.

Kira waves as Ken's truck pulls away. Ken is on his way to the dairy plant. Workers there will mix milk from Sunrise Farm with milk from other dairy farms.

Pipe Carrying Pasteurized Milk

Control Panel

Conveyor Belt

Automated Milk Carton Filler And Sealer

Dairy Worker

Before the milk can be sold, it must be tested to be sure it is fresh and pure. The milk is also pasteurized, a special process that kills any germs and keeps the milk fresh. Then the milk is poured into containers to sell in stores.

Jason leaves for town. At nine o'clock, Kira and Eve lead the cows out of the barn to the sunny pasture where they will eat green clover.

Then Kira goes to see the baby cows. Each one lives in its own little house in a special pen. First, Kira visits Polly, her own heifer.

"Good morning, Polly," says Kira. She looks at her proudly. Polly eats feed from Kira's hand. Then Kira feeds the other heifers.

Gate

Rail Fence

Heifer

Feeding Trough

As Kira leaves the pen, she forgets to close
the gate. The heifers are busy eating. Only one
notices the open gate.

Polly follows Kira into the great barn. Kira
has filled a bowl with milk and is looking for Cleo
the cat. Suddenly, she feels a push at her back.
She turns and sees Polly.

27

"Polly!" Kira says, with a laugh. "Did you come to help me with my chores? We'd better go back to your pen now."

Kira washes Polly. She brushes her. When she is finished, Kira closes the gate carefully. She looks at Polly. Kira hopes Polly will win a ribbon at the county fair later in the summer.

Silo

Hay

Hay
Mower

Tractor

Kira watches her mother in the tractor
cutting alfalfa hay.

Later Jason returns with the feed. Then he
checks the corn field. He will store the corn in
the silo, to be used as winter feed for the cows.

At five o'clock, the family leads the cows back into the great barn. They begin the evening milking. This time Kira helps her father, as Eve goes to the house to cook dinner.

Weather Vane

Cupola

Silo

Loft

When they finish, Jason hands Kira the diary.
She thinks. Then she writes:

July 22—A good day at Sunrise Dairy Farm.
Polly looks great. I hope she wins a ribbon at the
fair. I just can't wait to hear her moo again
tomorrow!